j797.37
T375j

3 5674 03508658 7

KNAPP BRANCH LIBRARY
13330 CONANT
DETROIT, MI 48212
852-4283

DEC 01

KN

JET SKI

Luke Thompson

Children's Press
A Division of Grolier Publishing
New York / London / Hong Kong / Sydney
Danbury, Connecticut

Book Design: Michael DeLisio
Contributing Editor: Jeri Cipriano
Photo Credits: Cover © Tony Stone; pp. 4, 6, 10, 13, 16, 19, 20, 29, 30, 33, 34, 37, 38, 41 © Indexstock; pp. 9, 24, 26 © All Sport; pp. 23-24 © AP/Wide World Photos

Visit Children's Press on the Internet at:
http://publishing.grolier.com

Library of Congress Cataloging-in-Publication Data

Thompson, Luke.
    Jet Ski / by Luke Thompson.
    p. cm. — (Built for speed)
    Includes bibliographical references and index.
    ISBN 0-516-23161-8 (lib. bdg.) — ISBN 0-516-23264-9 (pbk.)
    1. Jet skiing—Juvenile literature. [1. Jet skiing.] I. Title. II.
Built for speed

GV840.J4 T46 2000
797.3'7 —dc21
                                        00-064329

Copyright © 2001 by Rosen Book Works, Inc.
All rights reserved. Published simultaneously in Canada.
Printed in the United States of America.
1 2 3 4 5 6 7 8 9 10 R 05 04 03 02 01

CONTENTS

The saltwater stings your eyes. But at this speed things go by very quickly. You don't want to close your eyes for even a second. If you do, you could lose your balance and end up taking a spill. Look out! Better make way for that boat. You cruise in behind it. You jump over the waves the boat makes as it sails through the water. Time to break out some tricks. Try a barrel roll or a hurricane! Wave to your friends watching from the shore.

A jet ski is high-powered, fast excitement on the water. For thirty years, the sport of jet skiing has grown in popularity. Each year, more and more people cruise and skim the smooth waters of their local rivers, lakes, and oceans.

Jet skiing is high-powered excitement.

It takes a lot of practice to perform a trick like this on a jet ski.

If you like the water and the beach, then you might want to explore the sport of jet skiing. A jet ski lets you drive yourself at high speeds over water. Jet skis are fun and exciting. But jet skiing is not a sport for reckless daredevils. It's a sport that people of all ages can enjoy. Jet skiing can be as safe as it is thrilling. Whether you just want to cruise around for a day or soar at top speeds for an hour, jet skiing could be for you.

The History of
JET SKIING

Jet ski is really just a brand name, like Nike or Pepsi. What most people call a jet ski is actually called a personal watercraft (PWC). PWCs are boats that are used for recreation or sport racing. They are not made or sold for transportation or fishing. PWCs hold one to three people. Today, the name jet ski has come to represent all personal watercraft, not just those with the Jet Ski logo.

The jet ski was invented less than forty years ago. An inventor named Clayton Jacobsen II designed the first jet ski in his home in Arizona. He wanted to build a self-powered water ski that he could use on the lakes of his home state of Arizona.

Jacobsen's first jet ski was a cross between a motorcycle, a speedboat, and a jet aircraft. Like a motorcycle, Jacobsen's jet ski was steered using handlebars. Like a motorboat, it was made to travel very quickly across water. Finally, the jet ski was powered by a unique system of jet propulsion.

JET PROPULSION

Most boats are powered by propellers. But jet skis cannot be used safely with these propellers. If the rider were to fall off, the propeller could cause serious injury as it continued to spin. Jacobsen understood this problem when he built the first jet ski. He needed to invent a different kind of propulsion system. He finally decided that jet propulsion would do as good a job as a propeller—and jet propulsion is safe for the rider.

Jacobsen used an impeller to power his jet ski. An impeller is a type of propeller that has

Water shoots out of the nozzle at the rear of the craft.

been fitted into a tunnel. The engine spins the impeller, which pulls water from the front of the jet ski. The impeller pressurizes the water inside the tunnel. When enough pressure is built up, the water shoots out of the tunnel through a nozzle at the rear of the craft. As the impeller continues to spin, the pressurized water continues to shoot out the back of the jet ski. The pressurized water is what moves the jet ski, not the impeller! Now the jet ski can be driven like any other boat. Drivers use a throttle to control the jet ski's speed.

Now different companies make jet skis.

Jet skis built for recreation can go as fast as 30 or 40 miles per hour (48 or 64 km/h). Jet skis built for competition are able to go 50 or 60 miles per hour (80 or 96 km/h). A jet ski's speed depends on the size of its engine.

THE FIRST JET SKIS

The public saw Jacobsen's first jet ski in the 1960s. A company named Bombardier bought

Jacobsen's invention and tried to sell it. They were not successful. Boating was just becoming popular for most people. A single-person watercraft was not useful for families. People wanted to be on boats in groups, not riding around one at a time.

In the early 1970s, Kawasaki bought the invention from Bombardier and introduced the Jet Ski watercraft. People were now used to boating. They owned boats that could carry several people. Now they wanted one that could be used for sport fun. Kawasaki was able to sell its jet ski. It became so successful that jet skis soon were seen on rivers, lakes, and oceans around the world.

JET SKIS AND WAVERUNNERS

Originally, Jacobsen invented two types of jet skis. Both were powered by jet propulsion. The difference was that a rider sat on one and stood on the other.

Kawasaki's first jet ski only allowed riders to stand. This jet ski was a platform with a long handlebar. To steer, the driver had to lean to one side or another. This jet ski really acted like a ski!

As time passed, many people found that riding while sitting was better. Sitting was safer, more stable, and more comfortable than standing. Eventually companies began to develop PWCs that could seat two and three riders. The PWCs that seat two or three riders are called waverunners. Waverunners are built more for recreation than for competition. The stand-up jet ski is still popular today and is used in most competitions. As the popularity of the sport continues to grow, so will the number of different types of personal watercraft.

Standing on a jet ski is a lot like water skiing.

Here are the two different kinds of PWC: the jet ski and the waverunner.

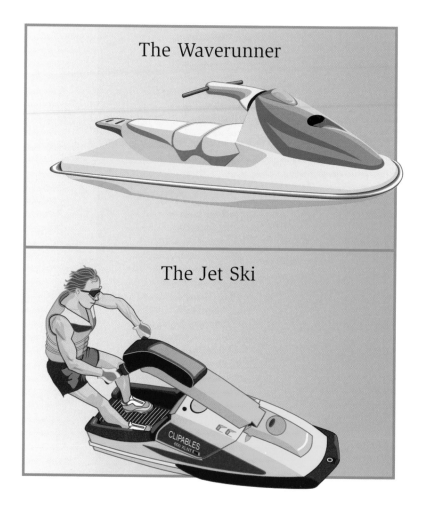

The Waverunner

The Jet Ski

Racing Jet
WATERCRAFT

Jet skis are built for speed and fun. Their design makes them perfect for racing. Almost as soon as the first jet skis were sold to the public, racing them became a sport. Their lightweight construction allows them to be fast and easily controlled. The jet ski is the most agile PWC on the market. That doesn't mean that jet skis are the only ones used for racing. Waverunners, even though they are built for recreation, are also exciting to race.

A day of organized jet-ski racing is called a watercross. Watercross events sometimes have twenty or more races. Jet watercraft racing is divided into different divisions. The type of racecourse and the boats that are used determine the different divisions. The ski

division is designed for jet skis only. The sport and runabout divisions are for waverunners. The difference between these two divisions is based on the size of the watercraft. The runabout division has larger, heavier boats than the sport division. The runabout division also requires that more than one person ride the craft.

SLALOM

The most popular style of jet-ski racing is the slalom event. The slalom event is held on a zigzag course. Riders start the race near the shore. When the flag drops, they race forward and weave in and out through floating markers. These buoys mark the slalom course over the water. The slalom race has two runs. There is a one-minute rest between each race. The rider with the fastest time for both races wins.

In an official slalom race, the course is 283 feet (80 m) long and is lined with nine buoys.

Jet-ski racers prepare for a slalom.

At each buoy the riders have to make a turn of some kind. The direction in which the riders must turn depends on the color of the buoy. A red buoy means turn left. A yellow buoy means turn right. Sometimes the turns are very sharp. Being able to maneuver these turns with speed and accuracy is the most important thing for racers.

FREESTYLE

Another major style of PWC racing is the freestyle competition. The freestyle event is not so much a race as it is a ballet on the water. In freestyle competitions, riders show their skill in performing creative tricks and difficult maneuvers. Each competitor gets two minutes to put together the best possible combination of tricks. The rider is then given a score between one and ten. One is the lowest score and ten is the highest. In an official freestyle competition, there are always seven

Freestyle jet-ski racers show their skill.

judges. Each judge gives a score to a rider. These scores are then added up and divided by seven to get the average score. The highest final score wins the competition.

There are dozens of different tricks one can do on a jet watercraft. Freestyle riders come up

with new tricks all the time. Here are six popular jet-ski tricks.

1 **The Tail Stand** This is a good trick for beginners. A rider must have good balance for this trick to work well. The driver pulls the nose (bow) of the jet ski into the air and holds it there as long as he or she can. Pulling a tail stand is a lot like popping a wheelie on a bike.

2 **The Barrel Roll** This trick is easy and a lot of fun. When a rider does a barrel roll, she rolls the jet ski over and dunks herself in the water. It's important that the rider doesn't let go when she is underwater, or the jet ski will be stuck upside-down.

3 **The Hurricane** This trick looks great, but it is very difficult. The hurricane takes twice the skill of doing a tail stand or a barrel roll. To do this trick right, a rider spins the jet watercraft around in

This rider is performing tricks on a jet ski.

tight circles. The challenging part of this trick is that the rider must take his foot off the ski. Only the most experienced riders should try the hurricane.

4 **Barefooting** This trick requires a rider to take both her feet off the ski. She swings one leg over so it is beside the other, and then she steps off, while the ski is still moving. Doing this trick while moving takes

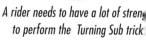

A rider needs to have a lot of strength to perform the Turning Sub trick.

a lot of time and practice. Barefooting also takes courage! Experienced barefoot riders can throw up an awesome spray of water using just their feet!

5 **The Turning Sub** To do the turning sub, a rider needs a lot of weight or strength. If the rider isn't heavy, he or she can learn to use the force of the jet ski to do this trick.

While moving, the rider must push the jet ski all the way under the water. First the nose will go underwater. The rider follows. Once under water, the rider has to be able to turn the jet ski. The end result is that the watercraft comes out from under the water going in a different direction than when it went under. Professional freestyle riders can make this trick look easy even though it is not.

6 **The Fountain** The fountain is a display trick. A rider shifts her balance toward the front of the watercraft while it is in motion. For a moment the nose may go underwater. This move kicks up the rear end (stern) and makes the jet ski shoot water into the air. The rider has turned her jet ski into a water fountain!

These riders are competing in a watercross race on a channel.

Watercrosses are really exciting to watch. The IJSBA Watercross Nationals takes place in different locations around the United States. Round one is held in Ft. Walton Beach, Florida. Round two takes place in Macon, Georgia. There are a total of eight rounds in the 2000 IJSBA Nationals. Some of the states that host this competition include California, Illinois, Missouri, New York, Texas, and West Virginia. The finals for 2000 were held in Chicago, Illinois.

These competitions are as exciting for the audience as they are for the riders. Watercross races are like a day at the beach. People pack lunches and sit on the sand to watch the competition. The roar of the jet skis and waverunners builds the excitement as the racers zoom away from the beach. Watercross courses are close to shore, which gives all the beach-bound fans a great view of the action.

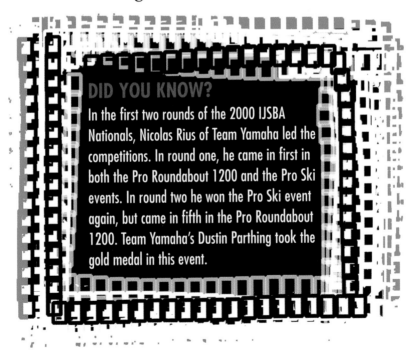

DID YOU KNOW?

In the first two rounds of the 2000 IJSBA Nationals, Nicolas Rius of Team Yamaha led the competitions. In round one, he came in first in both the Pro Roundabout 1200 and the Pro Ski events. In round two he won the Pro Ski event again, but came in fifth in the Pro Roundabout 1200. Team Yamaha's Dustin Parthing took the gold medal in this event.

Recreation and
EDUCATION

Jet skiing is a sport that can be enjoyed by people of all ages and abilities. Some day you might want to rent a jet ski and try the sport for yourself.

The experience of jet skiing is a unique feeling. It is much like riding a motorcycle, but less dangerous because jet skiing is done on water. Falling off a motorcycle can be deadly. Falling off a jet ski is less risky. Water cushions the fall so jet ski riders don't need to worry as much about injury.

Falling from a jet ski, however, can be frightening. No one should go out on the water without being aware that falling off a jet ski is likely. As long as a rider follows basic safety rules, he or she will be safe.

It takes a lot of skill to maintain balance on a jet ski.

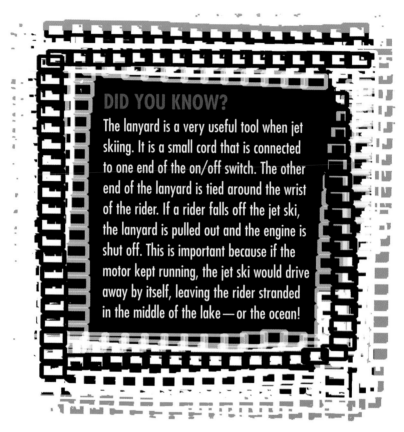

DID YOU KNOW?

The lanyard is a very useful tool when jet skiing. It is a small cord that is connected to one end of the on/off switch. The other end of the lanyard is tied around the wrist of the rider. If a rider falls off the jet ski, the lanyard is pulled out and the engine is shut off. This is important because if the motor kept running, the jet ski would drive away by itself, leaving the rider stranded in the middle of the lake—or the ocean!

The average jet watercrafts only run up to 40 or 45 miles per hour (64 or 72 km/h). Forty miles per hour on the water feels a lot faster than it does on the highway. You get this feeling of speed because you are so close to the water.

Jet skiers love to go fast.

Jet skis used in competition can run up to 70 miles per hour (112 km/h). Competition jet skis are not toys. Operating a racing jet ski is dangerous and should be left to the pros.

KNOW YOUR EQUIPMENT

To fully enjoy jet skiing, a rider needs to stay safe. The best way to stay safe is to know your watercraft and the equipment needed to ride it.

The jet ski is not the only piece of watercraft equipment about which you need to know. The most important piece of equipment

is the life jacket. A life jacket is a personal flotation device (PFD). A PFD is worn like a vest. It is made of foam rubber and is brightly colored to attract attention. A PFD is designed to keep a person's head above water after a fall. This is important for any water sport because a PFD keeps a person safe even if he or she is knocked unconscious.

A rider must wear a PFD while riding any kind of personal watercraft. This is the law. Anyone who jet skis without a PFD is running the risk of arrest as well as the risk of injury.

Other pieces of equipment that are recommended are wet suits, gloves, eye protection, and footwear. None of these is required, but using them helps riders in many ways. Wet suits are made to keep you warm. If you plan on using a jet ski in the northern United States, the water will be cold until the hottest part of summer. A wet suit lets you stay in the water for hours. Gloves protect the hands from

Jet-ski riders must always wear their life jackets.

blisters. Footwear, such as rubber surf shoes, protects your feet from sharp rocks while you get your jet ski in and out of the water.

Eye protection is one of the most important items on this list. There is nothing worse than getting struck in the eye while trying to control a watercraft at 40 miles per hour (64 km/h). Sunglasses may work, but goggles are the most effective protection for the eyes.

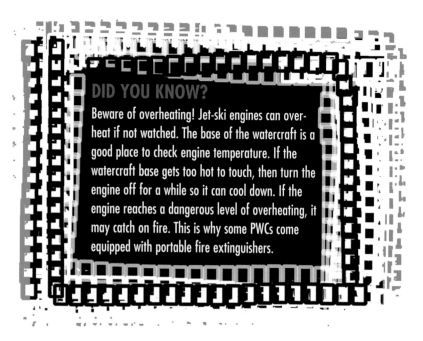

DID YOU KNOW?

Beware of overheating! Jet-ski engines can overheat if not watched. The base of the watercraft is a good place to check engine temperature. If the watercraft base gets too hot to touch, then turn the engine off for a while so it can cool down. If the engine reaches a dangerous level of overheating, it may catch on fire. This is why some PWCs come equipped with portable fire extinguishers.

Safety gear such as goggles and helmets are important and should be worn by all riders.

Jet Ski
SAFETY

The U.S. Coast Guard classifies all forms of jet watercraft as Class A boats. This classification means that a driver must be in command of the craft at all times. If the jet ski slips out from under a driver and injures someone else, the driver will be responsible for that accident.

Staying safe while jet skiing is a simple matter of following the rules and using your head. Here are the most important rules and regulations you need to know before using a jet watercraft:

To operate a PWC, a rider must have a valid driver's license and be at least sixteen years old. This is the recommendation of the Personal Watercraft Industry Association (PWIA). Rental businesses won't let a person

Safety guides help people enjoy the ride on a jet ski.

take out a jet ski without a valid license.

A PWC must be registered before you take it on the water. When a watercraft is registered, it receives an identification number. Identification numbers are just like license plate numbers. They are used in case of an accident or if someone is driving recklessly. Reporting an accident or a reckless driver is the right thing to do. Get your jet ski registered before you put it in the water.

As mentioned in the last chapter, the law requires that you wear a U.S. Coast Guard-approved PFD that fits properly. Life jackets save lives and wearing one is the most important rule in riding a PWC.

When driving a jet watercraft of any kind, using alcohol or drugs is strictly forbidden. The penalty for breaking this law is the same as for a person driving a car while intoxicated. The influence of drugs and alcohol makes the sport of jet skiing deadly.

It is not hard to find places to rent jet skis.

It is not just the driver who is endangered when he or she drinks. It is also everyone else on the water. The U.S. Coast Guard's advice is, "Be a sober skipper." This advice should be followed so that everyone on the water can have fun.

Lastly, it is important to be aware of local restrictions. There are a lot of waterways in the United States that do not allow PWCs. There are even more areas that have speed limits. The most common restriction you will find is "No Wake." The wake is the waves created behind a boat as it moves in the water. A "No Wake" zone means that all boats must go slowly because their wake could be damaging to the shore or to other boats. If you don't know about the local laws, ask a local official before you hit the water.

Jet skiing can be fun for anyone who is willing to give it a try. It is a sport that can be enjoyed at any speed. Different people ride jet skis for different reasons. Families ride jet skis

Jet skiing can be fun for everyone in the family.

for fun and to be together. Racers ride jet skis for competition and fame. The next time you're at the beach or on a lake, give it a try. Who knows? Maybe one today you'll be able to race a slalom course.

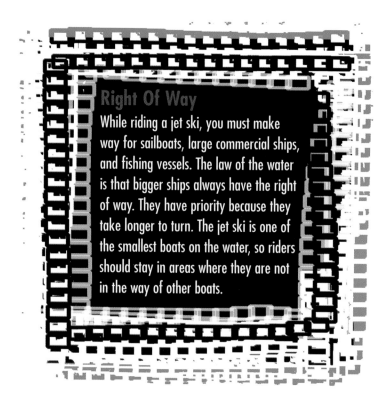

Right Of Way

While riding a jet ski, you must make way for sailboats, large commercial ships, and fishing vessels. The law of the water is that bigger ships always have the right of way. They have priority because they take longer to turn. The jet ski is one of the smallest boats on the water, so riders should stay in areas where they are not in the way of other boats.

Jet skiing is a good way for families to spend time together.

buoy a plastic ball or cone that is tied to the bottom of the lake and marks a slalom course

freestyle a competition in which riders do as many tricks as possible in a limited amount of time

impeller a propeller that is set inside the body of a watercraft

jet propulsion the kind of power used in jet watercraft

lanyard a safety cord tied to the jet ski's on/off button and the driver's wrist

personal watercraft any sort of small boat, such as a jet ski, that is meant for recreation and is ridden by one or two people

PFD a personal flotation device that is also known as a life jacket

slalom the typical form of racing for jet watercraft; it involves riding in a zigzag pattern through a buoyed race course

turning sub a trick in which the driver puts the watercraft underwater and turns it at the same time

For Further READING

Hawks, Nigel. *Ships and Other Sea Craft*. Brookfield, CT: Millbrook Press, 1999.

Italia, Bob. *Jet Skiing*. Minneapolis, MN: ABDO Publishing Company, 1992.

Leonard, Barry, ed. *Personal Watercraft Safety*. Upland, PA: DIANE Publishing Company, 2000.

RESOURCES

Web Sites

IJSBA—Jet Sports Racing

www.ijsba.com
This is the official site of the
International Jet Sports Boating
Association. Check out this site to learn
about event schedules, race results, and
competitors. You'll also find the IJSBA
official competition rulebook.

Personal Watercraft Illustrated—Online

www.watercraft.com
This is the official site of *Personal Watercraft
Illustrated* magazine. It provides information
about PWC racing, such as race results,
competitor profiles, and racing news.

RESOURCES

Organizations

American Watercraft Association
27142 Burbank
Foothill Ranch, CA 92610
Phone: (949) 598 5860
Fax: (949) 598 5872
www.watercraftassociation.com

Personal Watercraft Industry Association (PWIA)
Personal Watercraft Industry Association
1819 L. Street NW, Suite 700
Washington, DC 20036
Phone: (202) 721-1621
Fax: (202) 721-1626
www.pwia.org

INDEX

INDEX

About the Author

Luke Thompson was born in Delaware. He holds a degree in
English literature from James Madison University. He lives in
Vail, Colorado.